THE BEAT IN MY HEAD

ARIEL & BRANDON BLACKWELL

ILLUSTRATED BY SAM ONCHE

The Beat in My Head
Text Copyright © 2022 Ariel & Brandon Blackwell
Illustrations Copyright © 2022 Ariel & Brandon Blackwell

All rights reserved. No part of this book may be reproduced, distributed, or used in any form, including adaptation for publication, film, television, or any other media, without the prior written permission of the copyright holders. For permissions and inquiries, please visit thebeatinmyhead.com.

Second Edition Published by Sound World Productions LLC in 2025
254 Chapman Rd, Ste 208 #21523, Newark, Delaware 19702

Hardcover ISBN: 979-8-9937916-0-9
Ebook ISBN: 979-8-9937916-1-6
Library of Congress Control Number: 2025923385

To children all over the world—
God has placed something special inside you,
a gift only you can give to the world.

Your dreams are the seeds of your future.
Hold tight to them, have faith in your journey, and believe
that with love, courage, and God's grace, anything is possible.

—Ariel & Brandon Blackwell

In class, the teacher was writing on the board, and the chalk made a fantastic beat.

Tept shhh shh. Shhhhh. Tept Shh Shh. Tept shhh shhh. Shh shhh.

I started repeating it on my desk with my pencil. I enjoyed it so much that I got a little loud . . .

Hmmmm . . .

Hmmmm . . .

My teacher had enough. "Brandon, you must STOP distracting the class with your humming and tapping."

She called my mom. "Brandon's not paying attention at all."

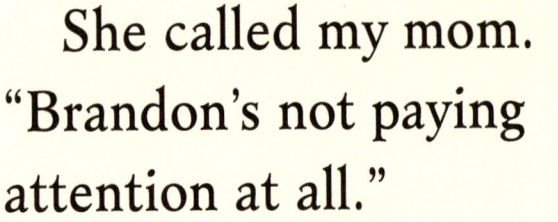

"I'm not trying to get distracted," I tried to explain. "I just can't stop the beat in my head."

My mom worried something more might be wrong because I didn't talk much or have many friends.

I didn't think anything was wrong with me.
I just loved music, and it loved me back.
It's my safe place. It was my best friend.

My mom wasn't so sure. So she took me to see a therapist.

He was friendly, but I didn't want to talk to him, so I played with the blocks on the rug and turned them into a keyboard.

Plink-a-plink-a-plink-a-plink.

"Brandon seems fine, just a little shy," he told my mom. "Maybe try sports. He can make new friends, and I'm sure the distracting music will stop."

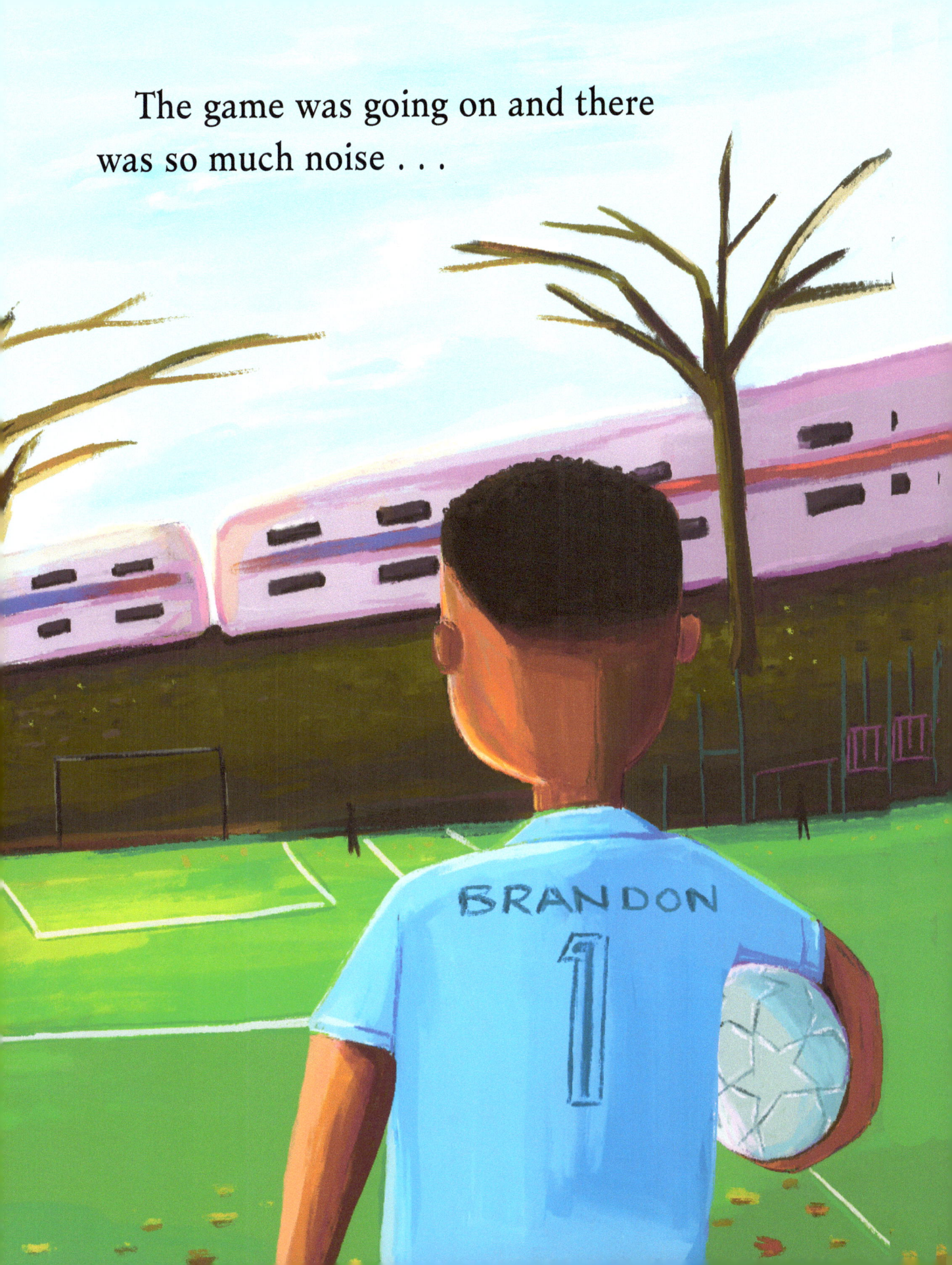

The game was going on and there was so much noise . . .

I heard a bird, and the sound was so beautiful. I closed my eyes and hummed along.

Chirp-Chirp. Tweet-Tweet. Chirp-Chirp.

Then, I got hit in the face.

That was the end of soccer.

We tried new things to keep me focused.

Karate—
but the kicks went *smack, smack, smack.*

Golf—but the clubs hitting the balls went *thwack, thwack, thwack.*

Even book club—
but the pages went *swish, swish, swish.*

Mom decided we should take a break and have some fun.
So she took me to a concert.

Mom and I swayed to the sounds of the instruments and sang the songs we knew.

I spotted a man off the stage who looked focused and bobbed his head along to the beat.
"Mom, what's that guy doing?" I asked.
"That's an audio engineer," she said. "He blends and balances the music to make the band sound good."

"I want to learn more about that," I said.

Then, I spent the rest of the show watching the audio engineer.

The following Sunday at church, my mom and I climbed the stairs to the balcony. She opened the door, and I saw speakers, lights, buttons . . .

and Mr. Davis.

He was the audio engineer for my church. My mom told him I was interested in his work, and he wanted to meet me.

"Want to check out the console?" he asked.

There was no music on, but I saw Mr. Davis tapping his foot.

"Do you hear music and sound in your head too?" I asked.

"Of course," he said. "There's nothing wrong with that. We're creatives."
I smiled. I am a creative.

Mr. Davis taught me all about the console every Sunday. I hummed and tapped along to the beat.

BRANDON and **ARIEL BLACKWELL** are a husband-and-wife author team inspiring kids worldwide through rhythm, creativity, and heart. They created The Beat In My Head to spotlight audio engineering and show children that music—and the people behind it—can change lives. **BRANDON BLACKWELL** is a live, studio, and broadcast audio engineer who has worked in sound since age nine. He has worked with many of today's biggest performers and is the Founder and CEO of Blackwell Productions. His work has been featured in Rolling Stone and other leading entertainment outlets. **ARIEL BLACKWELL** has worked with global companies and is a storyteller who empowers children to dream big. Together, they champion confidence, imagination, and every child's gift.

Learn more at www.thebeatinmyhead.com & www.brandonblackwell.com

SAM ONCHE is an illustrator/painter based in the United States. He was born in Nigeria, Benue, and moved to the US in 2015. He studied studio art at Colby College with a focus in oil painting. Sam uses the digital and oil medium to create illustrations for books, posters, prints, cover art, and album covers.

www.ingramcontent.com/pod-product-compliance
Lightning Source LLC
Chambersburg PA
CBHW051513110526
44582CB00008B/155